WE CAN SAVE THE EARTH

THE WATER WE DRINK

Written by:
Jill Wheeler

Published by Abdo & Daughters, 6535 Cecilia Circle, Edina, Minnesota 55439

Library bound edition distributed by Rockbottom Books, Pentagon Tower, P.O. Box 36036, Minneapolis, Minnesota 55435

Library of Congress Number: 90-083601   ISBN: 1-56239-002-3

Cover Illustrated by: C.A. Nobens
Interiors by: Kristi Schaeppi

Edited by: Stuart Kallen

TABLE OF CONTENTS

INTRODUCTION

Water is our most precious resource. It makes up more than 65 percent of our bodies. Humans can survive only a few days without water. In fact, all living things would die without water.

We use water for many things. We use it for drinking, washing, cleaning our clothes and homes, preparing our meals and growing our food. The average American uses about 60 gallons of water each day. Industries use even more water to manufacture things, to generate electricity, and to transport people and products.

Our water resources are *finite* — that means we have only what we have now, we cannot create more. Of all the water on earth, only 1 percent is suitable for drinking. Ninety-seven percent is salt water in the oceans. Two percent is frozen near the North and South poles.

Drinkable water comes from only a few places: surface waters, such as rivers, lakes and streams; and underground reservoirs called *aquifers*. More than 95 percent of the water people use comes from these aquifers. This water is called *groundwater*.

Often, water that is not good for drinking looks just like water that is good to drink. This is because many of the pollutants in our water are invisible chemicals. Sometimes these chemicals cannot be tasted or smelled, either. This causes many problems because people can get sick drinking water that tastes, smells and looks all right.

With so many people relying on just 1 percent of the water on earth, it only makes sense to preserve that water. Unfortunately, people are polluting and wasting the water we drink. The more water that is polluted and wasted, the less there is to use.

In this book, we will see how people are polluting the water we drink and how that pollution affects us. We'll also find out what we can do to help conserve our water resources and limit additional pollution.

CHAPTER 1
Pure to Polluted — A History of Water

The water we drink is as old as the earth, or about 4.5 billion years old. It has been used by countless other humans, animals and plants before us.

Scientists are unsure how water was created. Many believe water was at the center of the earth billions of years ago. It was so hot inside the earth that the water was in its vapor form, which is called steam. The steam came to the surface of the earth through vents in the earth's crust. Today, we call these vents *volcanoes, geysers,* and *hot springs.*

About one million years ago, the earth's climate became much colder. The water on the earth froze into giant sheets of mile-thick ice, called *glaciers.* As these glaciers moved slowly across the land, they created the landscape we know today.

When the earth began to warm, the glaciers melted. Lakes formed in the holes that the glaciers had scraped in the earth. Other water created the oceans. Over the centuries, rain water soaked into the earth to become groundwater.

Water from the glaciers was very pure. It had some pollutants, such as soil and plant material, but these were not harmful to living things.

Water pollution began when humans started dumping their waste into rivers, streams, and oceans to get rid of it. Dumping was the easiest and cheapest way to get rid of it.

At first, there was so little waste that it was not harmful. As more people lived on the earth, however there was more waste in the water. Eventually, there was not enough water to dilute the waste enough to make it harmless.

To make things worse, people began dumping very harmful chemicals, called *toxics*, into the water. There are many kinds of toxics. They are found in herbicides, pesticides, oil, household cleaners and many other things. If people eat or drink something with toxics in it, they can become very sick and may die.

The problem of toxics in water first was recognized in the late 1950's. At that time, many people around Minamata Bay in Japan began to get sick. Some lost control of their arms and legs. Others went deaf and blind. Still others died.

Doctors discovered the people were suffering from mercury poisoning. A nearby factory was dumping wastes into the water, including mercury. The mercury had been eaten by fish. People became sick when they ate the mercury-tainted fish.

Mercury is just one kind of heavy metal. Heavy metals, which include cadmium and lead, cause sickness and brain damage in humans. Heavy metals get into the body through air, food and water. They also can harm children even before they are born.

In the United States, the problem of toxics became so bad near Cleveland, Ohio, that in June 1969, the Cuyahoga River burst into flames. Normally water cannot burn — it is used to put out fires. Factories near the Cuyahoga had dumped so many pollutants, including oil, into the river that it caught fire, causing much damage.

Ten years later, thousands of people in the Love Canal neighborhood of Niagara, New York, had to leave their homes. It was discovered that hazardous waste had been buried in their neighborhood for more than 20 years and was contaminating their water. The bad water was causing people in that neighborhood to suffer increased rates of cancer, as well as a high number of miscarriages and birth defects.

Thousands of people in Pennsylvania and West Virginia had to buy bottled water because a huge diesel fuel spill contaminated the Monongahela River in November 1987. In 1989, a supertanker dumped 11 million gallons of crude oil into Prince William Sound in Alaska, killing thousands of fish, birds and other wildlife.

These examples are highly visible effects of water pollution. Other areas of pollution are just as bad but not as well known. New waste sites are discovered virtually every day. In the next chapter, we will see why.

Did You Know . . .

Only 10 percent of the toxic waste generated by American industry each year is diposed of safely.

CHAPTER 2
Water Today

In 1988, many parts of the United States suffered from the most severe drought in more than 50 years. Grass, trees and shrubs withered and died. People and animals suffered in the heat. Some of them died. Many people wondered if there would ever be enough water again.

Even though the drought ended, there still is valid concern about where we will get enough clean, drinkable water. As our population grows, so does our demand for water. But our water resources are limited, unlike our population growth.

In the United States, we use about 450 billion gallons of water each day. Most of that water comes from surface waters and aquifers. Both of these sources are easily polluted, as you will see:

We harm the water we drink when we spray pesticides on our lawns and dump hazarous wastes like motor oil, paints and household chemicals on the ground. All of these pollutants filter down through the soil, eventually reaching aquifers.

We harm the water we drink when we send garbage to landfills. Harmful chemicals in our waste seep through the ground in the land fill and end up in groundwater. One landfill alone is estimated to leak four million gallons of toxic liquids a day into nearby streams.

We harm the water we drink when we operate appliances that run on electricity. Power plants use water to cool their equipment. When the plants return the water, it is much warmer. Warm water cannot hold as much oxygen as cool water. This oxygen shortage harms the fish and plants that live in the water. Warm water also encourages bacteria, which makes people sick.

We harm the water when we use paper, steel, processed food, synthetic fabrics and chemicals. These industries are among the worst polluters. They dump many manufacturing by-products into the water. These pollutants include oil, acids, wood chips, metal, animal parts, dyes, salt and plastics. These industries also use large quantities of water for generating electricity and cooling and cleaning equipment.

We harm the water when we overwater our lawns, wash our cars every week and leave the water running. All of these activities waste water. Remember, we only have 1 percent to use!

We harm the water when we flush wastes down the toilet. More than 189 million tons of solid waste are legally dumped into the oceans each year. The waste comes from pipes called ocean-*outfalls*, which drain sewage directly into the ocean.

We harm the water when we buy products grown with agricultural chemicals, irrigation, or crops grown on drained wetlands. Substances like pesticides, herbicides and fertilizers wash off farmland and contaminate groundwater. Irrigation systems drain away scarce water. Wetlands clean water by filtering out sediment and trapping many harmful chemicals. But America is losing wetlands at the rate of 300,000 acres per year.

Humans are doing many things to harm the water we drink. There also are many things we can do to clean dirty water and conserve clean water. The next chapter shows how.

Did You Know . . .

Just one quart of motor oil can contaminate 250,000 gallons of water.

The Environmental Protection Agency has identified more than 700 toxic compounds in samples drawn from U.S. water systems.

Up to one-fourth of the world's water supply could be unsafe by the year 2000.

CHAPTER 3
What You Can Do

Everyone can conserve water and reduce water pollution every day by following a few simple steps. Read on for some water-saving ideas:

Save Water at Home

- Don't leave the water running when you brush your teeth or wash dishes or food. Use a tub of soapy water to wash dishes, and turn the faucet on halfway to rinse. You can waste a gallon of water in just 60 seconds with the water on full blast.

- Don't use the kitchen sink as a waste dump. Everything you send down the drain may go to a water treatment plant and end up back in your tap. If you must use hazardous chemicals such as household cleaners, paint or solvents, store them in tightly closed containers until they can be taken to a hazardous household waste collection point.

- Put a quart bottle filled with water in your toilet tank to use less water per flush. One bottle can save up to 15 percent of the water you use to flush each day.

- Keep a bottle of drinking water in the refrigerator. That way, you won't have to run the tap water until it gets cold.

- Watch what you eat. It takes 2,500 gallons of water to produce one pound of beef, and 408 gallons of water to produce one serving of chicken. Vegetables take much less water to produce.

Did You Know . . .

The water used by just one person in a year would cover a football field four feet deep.

- Check your detergents for phosphates. Phosphates kill lakes and streams by encouraging algae and bacteria growth. Use low-phosphate or phosphate-free detergents. Most soap packages tell if the detergent is phosphate-free. Use less detergent overall. Many detergent manufacturers recommend using more than is necessary.

- Clean latex paint-filled brushes indoors where the wastewater can go to a water treatment facility rather than directly into the ground.

- Fix leaks. One leaky faucet can waste more than 50 gallons of water a day. A leaky toilet wastes 750 gallons of water a month.

Did You Know . . .

Up to 35 percent of the world's land surface is threatened with becoming a desert due to water depletion.

- Take a shower instead of a bath. Showers use one-third less water than baths.

- Recycle. The less garbage that goes to the landfill, the less chance there is of water contamination from that garbage.

Did You Know . . .

Toilets use 40 percent of all household water. Showers and baths are second at 20 percent.

The price of water has increased up to 37 percent in some American cities in the last two years.

Save Water Outside

- Use a soaker hose instead of a lawn sprinkler. Water lawns in the evening or early morning to reduce evaporation.

- Wash your car at home rather than a car wash. A trigger nozzle on the hose will save another 20 gallons of water each time.

- Avoid using lawn chemicals. Instead, leave the grass clippings on the lawn for natural fertilizer, and supplement it with organic fertilizers.

Did You Know . . .

Between 50 and 80 percent of the water used to water the lawn is lost to evaporation, seepage and street runoff.

• Sweep sidewalks and driveways rather than using the garden hose. You'll save hundreds of gallons of water.

Save Water at School

- Ask your school to install low-flow shower heads and faucets. Low-flow shower heads reduce water consumption by 50 percent.

- Urge your school to use organic lawn methods. The poisons used on lawns can make people and animals sick.

- Work with your classmates to write letters to lawmakers urging them to pass stricter clean water laws.

Did You Know . . .

Water use in the U.S. increased from 180 billion gallons a day in 1950 to 450 billion gallons in 1980.

A FINAL WORD

Before reading this book, you may have thought that our supply of water was never ending. As you've found out, however, there is a limited supply of water on the earth. As more people realize this fact, they are doing more things to protect our most precious natural resource.

This book is full of helpful hints on how to conserve water. If you follow even a few of these suggestions, you will save hundreds of gallons of water a year. Encourage others to follow your example. By conserving water now, you'll make sure that there will be plenty of clean water for your children and grandchildren.

GLOSSARY

AQUIFER: A layer of rock, sand or gravel in the earth that holds water.

BACTERIA: Very tiny plants that can only be seen through a powerful microscope.

BY-PRODUCT: A product that comes from the making of something else.

CONSERVE: To protect and wisely use forests, rivers, minerals and other natural resources.

CONTAMINATE: To make dirty; to pollute.

DILUTE: To make thin or weaker by adding a liquid.

DROUGHT: A long period of time when there is very little rain or no rain at all.

EVAPORATE: To change from a liquid or solid into gas.

FERTILIZER: A substance that is added to soil to make it better for growing of crops.

GEYSER: A hot spring from which steam and hot water shoot into the air.

GLACIER: A large mass of ice formed by snow that does not melt. A glacier moves slowly across land or down a valley.

GROUNDWATER: Water within the earth that supplies wells and springs.

HAZARDOUS WASTE: Waste that is dangerous to the health of people, animals or the environment.

HERBICIDE: A chemical substance used to destroy or stop plant growth.

HOT SPRING: A spring with water above 98 degrees Fahrenheit.

LANDFILL: An area built up by burying layers of trash between layers or dirt.

MERCURY: A heavy silver-colored metal.

ORGANIC: Having to do with or coming from living things; using or grown by farming or gardening methods in which chemicals are not used.

OUTFALL: The mouth of a body of water, drain or sewer.

OXYGEN: A gas that has no color or smell. Oxygen makes up one-fifth of the air on earth.

PESTICIDE: A chemical substance used to destroy bugs and other pests.

PHOSPHATE: A poisonous chemical element.

POLLUTANTS: Man-made wastes found in the air, ground and water.

RECYCLE: Reusing materials instead of wasting them.

SEDIMENT: Small pieces of matter that settle at the bottom of a liquid.

SYNTHETIC FABRIC: Material that is man-made.

TOXIC: Of, relating to or caused by poison.

VOLCANO: An opening in the surface of the earth through which lava, gasses and ashes are forced out.

WETLANDS: Land or areas that contain much soil moisture.

INDEX

DATE DUE		
JAN 22 1991 MAR 2 9 1994		
OCT 7 '91 fac 207		
DEC 18 92		
P. Thomas Wetmore		
JAN 3 0 '95		
FEB 28 '95		
MAR 24 '95		
OCT 02 '95		
OCT 09 '95		
APR 0 6 1997		

1226

363   Wheeler, Jill.
WHE   The water we drink.